FAMOUS BRAND NAMES, EMBLEMS AND TRADE-MARKS

Marjorie Stiling

DAVID & CHARLES
Newton Abbot   London   North Pomfret (Vt)

British Library Cataloguing in Publication Data

Stiling, Marjorie
    Famous brand names, emblems and trademarks
    1. Trademarks – Great Britain
    2. Business names – Great Britain
    I. Title
    602'.75   T257.V2

    ISBN 0–7153–8098–2

Printed in Great Britain
by Biddles Limited, Guildford, Surrey
for David & Charles (Publishers) Limited
Brunel House, Newton Abbot, Devon

Published in the United States of America
by David & Charles Inc.,
North Pomfret Vermont 05053 USA

Contents

Introduction

'Make your mark,' was my grandfather's pet theme. 'Look around—note all those who've left their mark!' And before I realised what he had really meant, I had latched on to advertisements, and was well into trademarks. I wondered how some of the most familiar trademarks and emblems were chosen. What made them famous?

To have one's trademark recognised throughout the world as a symbol of reliability must surely be every tycoon's dream. Many marks are self-explanatory. But what connection has a kiwi bird with shoe polish, a shell with petrol, or a crusader with the *Daily Express*? And how do carnations relate to corn caps?

Emblems and symbols as used by some professionals and organisations also raise the same questions. So some are included—as also are some advertising symbols which, due to magazine, press, and particularly television exposure, have become as well known or even better known than their firm's registered trademark.

But this book is not intended to be a mere list of trademarks and emblems which most of us can see for ourselves. In it I have tried to relate how the symbols came to be chosen, where, when, and by whom; to tell a little of the stories behind the symbols and, in some cases, something of the lives and genius of the men who created them.

I approached the heads of various firms and organisations and their public relations officers, and received much fascinating information. I am indebted to them for their generous co-operation.

It is only possible, of course, to mention a fraction of the many well-known brand names, emblems and trademarks that exist, but from this selection it is easy to see why their owners are proud of them and jealously guard them from piracy.

Marjorie Stiling
Exmouth 1980

adidas

A survey by this German company's management a few years ago showed that 80% of all West Germans between the ages of 16 and 69 knew what the word 'adidas' stood for. But it is doubtful if the figure would be so high in other countries—even though 'adidas' (always with a lower case 'a') can be seen almost everywhere, particularly on attention-grabbing sports bags.

Its story began in 1948 in the small Bavarian mill town of Herzogenaurach. As a result of a quarrel between Rudolf Dassler and his brother Adolf (Adi), Rudolf left the family sports business to set up on his own. Adolf, using the three letters of his nickname and the first three letters of his surname, then changed the name of the existing firm. Today the name, and trefoil, are both registered trademarks.

The first samples of adidas footwear appeared at the Olympic Games in Helsinki in 1952, already marked with the now famous and eyecatching three stripes to which the trefoil was added later.

Adi Dassler died in 1978, aged 77, leaving a widow, a son, and four daughters, but in preparation for the inevitable he had carefully groomed his successors. What has become the largest producer of sports goods in the world today is still a family-owned company. The family all live close to one another in and around Herzogenaurach, meeting informally, as well as in the factory every day.

Aquascutum

In London in 1851 there was a small, high-quality tailor's shop in Regent Street. While continuing to make magnificent suits and overcoats, the company was trying to do something that had never been done before—to produce wool that was showerproof.

It was reasoned that, on a sheep, the natural oil in its wool gave better protection than an umbrella, but in the interests of clean living, these oils had of necessity to be removed before the wool could be woven into cloth. The resulting cloth garment left its wearer at the mercy of a shower of rain.

The company tried many additives to replace the oil and, in 1853, John Emary perfected the process. Immediately, from two Latin words meaning water shield, the new, rain-repellent cloth acquired the name 'Aquascutum'. The very awkwardness of the sound created interest and visitors from Europe pronounced it in half-a-dozen different ways. From that small shop in 1851 sprang what was to become today one of Britain's great international names—Aquascutum.

Aspro

According to the memory of George Nicholas, the Melbourne pharmacist who first made Australian aspirin and later founded the Aspro business, the name ASPRO was a union of AS and PROforma—meaning the same product previously sold as Aspirin Nicholas. But years later, in January 1951, a boardroom minute recorded that ASPRO was an invented word having its origin in the fact that it was a Nicholas Product—the last two letters of the word NicholAS and the first three letters of the word PROduct.

The Aspro story began indirectly in 1915 when George Nicholas, a 31 year-old chemist, attempted to make aspirin. Until 1914 supplies had come from Germany, made by the Bayer Company who owned the trademark Aspirin worldwide. When Bayer stopped exporting to enemy states, the Australian Government cleared the way for home production. With the help of another chemist, Harry Shmith, success came in 1915. By 1916 George's brother Alfred had agreed to work with them.

But in 1917, an MP named W. H. Kelly claimed that the Nicholas brothers were a front for German interests. They were, in fact, Australian-born descendants of a British mining family from Cornwall. During this smear campaign George and Alfred invented, and in April 1917 registered, the trade name Aspro for their aspirin. So when, in the following July, the Government cancelled their right to the use of the name aspirin, the Nicholas team had already set off, with a branded name, in what was to prove a far better direction. Today, Nicholas International Limited, still a Melbourne-based business, has more than four-fifths of its income outside Australia.

Barclays Bank

The black spread eagle has been used as the emblem of Barclays Bank since the early days of banking in England when the bankers were goldsmiths.

In 1692, John Freame was a partner in a banking business which was carried on at premises in Lombard Street, under the sign of the Three Anchors. In 1728 he moved the firm into the adjacent building (No 56 Lombard Street) which he had bought with the sign of the Black Spread Eagle. John's sister married James Barclay who joined the partnership in 1736. Over the next 200 years the name of Freame's business changed many times as partners died and new partners joined, but the name of Barclay remained constant until the firm became the banking company of Barclay and Company in 1896.

As time passed, they acquired other properties in Lombard Street—The Three Crowns (No 43), the Three Kings (No 55) and The Bible (No 54). The banking partnership adopted 54 Lombard Street as their official address, but the sign of that house, The Bible, was not used. Instead, the partners continued to display the Black Spread Eagle.

Eventually Barclays Bank Limited sought a grant of arms. They wanted to keep the eagle but, because other ancient and royal houses carry it in various forms, the College of Arms ruled that he must be 'differenced'. This was done by putting on three crowns—appropriately since Nos 43 and 55 which bore the signs of the Three Crowns and the Three Kings were now part of the Head Office site. The grant of arms was officially made in 1937.

The sign outside 54 Lombard Street today is not the bank's official heraldic device; the black spread eagle is John Freame's original eagle without the crowns, and he faces outwards from the building from whichever side he is seen.

Bass

The label incorporating the world-famous Bass red triangle—originally a shipping mark—is the world's oldest registered trade mark. It had already been used officially by the company for twenty years when, in 1875, the Trade Marks Registration Act was introduced. A faithful member of the Bass staff, determined that the Bass label with the red triangle should hold the coveted No 1 place, is said to have spent an uncomfortable night on the steps of the registrar's office to make sure of being first in the office the following morning. His loyalty was rewarded; despite reported pushing in the registrar's hall, he also took registration No 2 with the Bass red diamond (traditionally associated with Burton Ale) and No 3 with the brown diamond for Porter and Extra Stout.

The company was founded in 1777 by William Bass, the owner of a carrying business between London and Manchester. His decision to establish his own brewery in Burton-upon-Trent was inspired by the amount of beer he was carrying for other brewers.

Later, William's son, Michael Thomas Bass, with other Burton brewers, developed a thriving export business in Eastern Europe and Russia; by 1800, Michael was trading with sixty seven merchant importers. This prosperous seaborne trade for the Burton brewers owed much to the Trent Navigation Act of 1699 and its later further development.

William Bass built a reputation for the quality of his beers which has been carried on by his descendants and retained since the Bass Charrington merger in 1967 (when the triangle trademark was slightly amended).

In 1977, the company's bicentenary year, the Bass Museum was founded and opened daily to the public. It is the country's first major museum devoted to the brewing industry.

Many forgeries of the Bass trademarks have been made; Bass has albums containing over 2,000 examples produced over the years in the hope of taking advantage of the fame of Bass Beers.

Beefeater Gin

Although this attractive trademark, which portrays a figure dressed in the Tudor period uniform of the Yeoman Warders of the Tower of London, was registered in 1910, it is understood that the firm started using the Beefeater name and figure in the 1890s. But how did this name and figure become related to gin?

The firm of distillers was originally founded in Cale Street, Chelsea, in 1820, but records for those early years are rather vague. In 1898, on the death of James Burrough, two of his three sons formed the firm into a limited liability company and looked for a trademark which was symbolic of London and synonymous with tradition, prestige and quality. They chose the nickname and uniform of the Yeoman Warders of the Tower of London. Today, the firm of James Burrough Limited, Distillers, export their Beefeater Gin to over 170 countries, and it is registered in 101 of them.

Birds Eye

There appears to be no record of why the albatross was chosen as the symbol for Birds Eye Foods. Its original design was created in the USA when, in the early 1930s, the General Foods Corporation acquired the freezing patent of Clarence Birdseye—a scientist who developed the technique of preserving food by quick freezing.

Clarence Birdseye was an American fur-buyer and biologist whose work took him into the wilds of Labrador. In the Arctic he noticed that frozen caribou meat and frozen fish tasted fresh-flavoured when thawed. But his scientific knowledge told him that normal freezing of meat or fish created large ice crystals which broke down the texture of the cell walls and consequently, on thawing, the result was a tasteless, soggy mess. He came to the conclusion that the secret lay in the speed with which the food was frozen. Food left exposed to the elements in the sub-zero temperatures of Labrador in winter froze solid in a matter of minutes. From this observation, Clarence Birdseye discovered that, during quick freezing, many thousands of tiny ice crystals are formed (instead of comparatively few large ones), and these did not affect the cell structure nor injure the food.

In 1926 he founded a company at Gloucester, Massachusetts, for the freezing of fish. But progress was slow. In 1929 he sold out to General Foods. About 1943, Unilever acquired the patent rights for the UK and the rest of the world outside the USA. Since 1943, when Birds Eye Foods went into production in the UK, the logotype albatross design has undergone several slight modifications.

Bostik

The Boston Blacking Company opened its first research laboratory in 1931. During experiments and development of a rubber latex adhesive for the shoe industry, it was discovered that a similar adhesive would not only stick rubber to metal, but was waterproof and resistant to vibration. From this discovery came the first Bostik product. The name BOSTIK was derived from BOSton and STIK from the word stick, though the Company did not change its name to Bostik Limited until 1962.

Bostik, as we know it today, was actually 'born' in 1898 when the Boston Blacking Company was established in Belvoir Street, Leicester. In 1902, the company manufactured its first rubber adhesives under the name of Herculean Cement, and during the First World War supplied the sewing waxes and other products used in the manufacture of Army boots. The discovery of Bostik in 1931 enabled the company's products to be used extensively in the Second World War on naval and merchant ships as well as land vehicles and aircraft. Special Bostik products were used for sealing aircraft and fuel tanks.

Today Bostik Limited, England, is part of the Bostik Chemical Group with operating units in twenty-three countries around the world, with facilities for research and development to keep up to date with technological progress.

Bovril

The name Bovril 'came to me over a cigar' said John Lawson Johnston when interviewed by a journalist in 1887. The name originated from BO—the Latin word for ox, and VRIL—from Vrilya, the name given to the life force in a novel called *The Coming Race* by Bulwer Lytton published in 1871.

John Lawson Johnston was born in 1839 in Roslin, Midlothian, and educated in Edinburgh. In his mid-thirties he emigrated to Canada where, after the starvation into surrender of Paris in the Franco-Prussian War of 1871, he won a contract from the French Government to supply canned meat to stock up the French forts against future emergencies. This enabled him to develop the blending of meat extract with other raw materials which he had already contemplated. The result, Johnston's fluid beef, the forerunner of Bovril, was first manufactured commercially in 1874 at Sherbrooke in the province of Quebec, and it proved so popular that the firm moved to a larger factory in Montreal in 1880. The product still sells in British Columbia under its original name.

Johnston returned to the United Kingdom in 1884 and from small beginnings at 10 Trinity Square, London, he developed the Bovril Company whose product was to sell and become a household name all over the globe. In its earliest advertisement (1889) the product was described as Johnston's Fluid Beef (brand Bovril). After that, it was simply called Bovril.

Bukta

Where is the value of an old painting without the signature? Where is your guarantee of any commodity without the trademark of a World-known House? These questions appeared in 1913 beneath instructions for washing Bukta football shirts and jerseys. Above the instructions was the picture of a highland stag. By 1960, the stag emblem had more aptly become the leaping buck. In 1971 this was changed to a more stylised buck, and slightly modified in 1976.

But the registered name Bukta which distinguishes sportswear throughout the world and camping equipment for Everest explorers, besides being the pet name for the Company itself, has remained constant for over 100 years. The name is derived from that of the man who started the business in a cellar in Portland Street, Manchester, in the 1870s with plant of about twelve treadle sewing machines—Edward Robinson Buck. In spite of early difficulties and limited resources, through his own enterprise and shrewd business acumen he slowly progressed. He brought up and educated thirteen children and, in 1907, took three of his sons into partnership.

Apart from being the originator of the printed-stripe football shirt, he forsaw the potentialities of the Boy Scout movement in its early days when most people scoffed and became their recognised official outfitter. At the Boy Scouts' World Jamboree at Birkenhead Park in 1929, the adjoining BUKTA Exhibition Camp was visited by Boy Scouts from all lands and though many of them could speak no English, they proudly pointed to the Bukta name-tabs on the uniforms they were wearing.

Camp Coffee

A red seal stamped with the words 'Camp Coffee' is the trademark registered by R. Paterson & Sons Limited, of Glasgow, Scotland, established in 1849. But it is the label used on Camp Coffee that has always raised interest—who was that Scots officer being served with a cup of coffee?

It is thought that the officer was probably drawn by an artist employed by the company's printers in Nottingham and that the model was Sir Hector MacDonald, a general in the Boer War. But only his head was used; the uniform was deliberately drawn to avoid portraying any particular regiment and also it was thought that to show a general might provoke ill-feeling in Sir Hector, and possibly action by the War Office.

In 1954, the Company did try to register the 'Highlander' alone, as a separate trademark, but the War Office would not allow a soldier in uniform to be registered as a trademark. The Company tried again a few years later, and the registration was accepted.

The motto—Ready aye Ready—as shown on the label, is fairly widely used in Scotland but not traceable as the actual motto of any particular family. It was a battle cry used by several clans such as the Johnstons, Stewarts, Napiers and Scotts, apparently confined mainly to South of Scotland families.

The label used nowadays is a very much changed variation of the label produced as long ago as 1883.

Carnation Corn Caps

There is a simple explanation why a seemingly humble commodity such as corn caps were given the name of these delicate flowers. 'Carnation' in the Oxford Dictionary is defined as 'Rosy pink (orig. flesh) colour'. This colour aptly describes the three constituent items of the finished product—the adhesive cloth, the medicated ointment, and the adhesive ring that relieves shoe pressure. But most important, the name of the colour allows alliteration—that is to say Carnation Corn Caps. This is simple to remember and slips easily off the tongue.

But there was nothing simple about the man who devised Carnation Corn Caps. Alfred William Gerrard was a genius. Few pharmacists ever accomplished so much in their lifetime, or contributed more to our knowledge of drugs and their chemical, pharmaceutical, and manufacturing processes This one-time chief pharmacist at University College Hospital, London, was also a founder member in 1878 of the Cuxson, Gerrard & Company which today, over a hundred years later, is still manufacturing Carnation Corn Caps.

Alfred Gerrard, at the age of 16, left his native Dorset for London. Three years later he became dispenser at Guys Hospital where he found opportunities for research. Sixty-seven papers published by Gerrard during the fifty years up to 1920 embodied the results of his inventive genius, important research and acute observations.

Of his many hundreds of achievements, 'plaster spreading' had attracted his attention at Guy's Hospital. He improved the spreading machine in use at the hospital, and the modified machine is still known by his name. His formula for 'Guy's lead plaster' was manufactured by him in the backyard of his own residence in Islington for the use of the German army during the Franco-German War.

The memory of Alfred William Gerrard is perpetuated by the striking of a gold medal awarded annually for distinction in pharmacy—Gerrard's special subject—at the

School of Pharmacy of Birmingham Central Technical College.

Corgi

Why was a little dog chosen to be the trademark for this die-cast model range of toys? The connection is easily explained; with the models being made in Swansea, South Wales, it was felt that the name of a Welsh dog which conjures up miniature, robust and pedigree, was very apt. Also corgi, being a two-syllable word, would be easy for children to say and remember. An added bonus was that the corgi has achieved its own special status being the breed of dog associated with the British Royal family.

The corgi brand name is acknowledged by the Mettoy Company as possibly their most important property; it has been in use since 1956 when the die-cast range was launched. It is now being applied to a number of other ranges, including die-cast scale models, electronic games, sonic-controlled cars, and walkie-talkies. All neat—yet as robust as the CORGI.

Courvoisier

Courvoisier 'The Brandy of Napoleon' was first registered as a trademark in 1909. But how did it get this name?

According to the French Historian André Castelot, Emperor Napoleon often had supplies of brandy from the Cognac region sent to him. A few bottles were always included in his baggage when he went on a campaign. After his abdication in July 1815, he thought of leaving secretly for the United States and, the Minister of Police, Fouché, arranged for two ships anchored in the little port of Fourras to be victualled. The provisions put on board included the best cognac of the area—especially selected by Emmanuel Courvoisier from Jarnac.

However, this escape project was quickly dropped and Napoleon decided to give himself up to the British. Consequently, he set sail for the island of Aix in the Atlantic opposite Rochefort where the *Bellérophon* was waiting for him. But Napoleon had too many possessions to transfer to it and a second ship, *Mirmidon*, had to be affreighted. On both these ships sailing as far as Plymouth, and then on HMS *Northumberland* sailing to St Helena, the British officers had many occasions to taste the Cognac brandy that had been especially selected by Emmanuel Courvoisier. They appreciated it so much that, later, they often spoke to their friends about the Emperor's Brandy. In this way, Courvoisier came to be known in English as 'The Brandy of Napoleon'.

Daily Express

The crusader on the top right-hand corner of the front page of the *Daily Express* (but top left-hand corner of the *Sunday Express*) is more than a mere imprint. It is the newspaper's symbol of faith—attributed to the late Lord Beaverbrook—from his Empire free trade crusade of the thirties, the *Daily Express's* faith in the British Empire and its devotion to the Empire cause.

The crusader first appeared on 29 March 1930, but during the years since then there have been slight changes in the symbol, reflecting the paper's feelings towards the British Government's Empire Policy

On 16 November 1932 the crusader appeared the first day without a coat of arms. On 26 September 1942 a dagger was shown on the crusader's shield. But the most significant change was shown on 15 October 1951—the crusader appeared in chains. The reason given was that the *Daily Express* had supported the Tories in the General Election in the belief that they would produce an Empire Policy and the *Express* was waiting expectantly, hopefully, for the moment when Tory principles in relation to the Empire were made clear. The crusader was not freed from his shackles until 14 September 1964. And 19 March 1973 saw new title type together with a new crusader, ever the *Daily Express's* symbol of faith.

Drambuie

The name Drambuie is coined from the Scottish Gaelic *dram* drink and *buidheach* satisfying, pleasing or *buidh* yellow, golden; in fact, the contraction of a Gaelic phrase 'an dram buidheach' which means 'the drink that satisfies'.

This liqueur has a romantic history. In 1746 after the Jacobite Prince Charles Edward Stuart (Bonnie Prince Charlie), Pretender to the throne of Great Britain, was defeated in battle at Culloden, he was hunted across the Highlands and Islands of Scotland with a price of £30,000 on his head. Flora MacDonald rowed with him, disguised as a serving maid, over to the Island of Skye where he was given refuge by John Mackinnon of Strathaird. Practically destitute, all the Prince could offer Mackinnon in thanks was his personal recipe of what was later to become known as Drambuie.

How the Prince himself came by the Drambuie recipe is not recorded, but from adolescence he had travelled the courts and drawing-rooms of Europe in pursuit of his ambition to restore the fortunes of his disposed Stuart family. It is certain that he became accustomed to a wide range of food and drink which must have given him considerable insight into the magics that charm the palate.

The Mackinnons of Skye kept the Prince's recipe a secret for 150 years—only sharing the royal dram that resulted from it with a few close friends. But these appreciative friends became so persuasive that in 1892 the Mackinnon family registered Drambuie as a trademark.

In 1906, Young Malcolm Mackinnon decided to produce Drambuie on a commercial scale in Edinburgh. Only one Mackinnon in each generation knows the recipe, though one written copy exists, locked in the vaults of an Edinburgh lawyer's office.

Today, Drambuie is obtainable in every country except Tibet—though even there it is possible that the occasional bottle finds its way across the Himalayan passes to offer a glimpse of wider horizons than those provided by fermented yak's milk.

Dulux Paint

The first Old English Sheepdog identified with Dulux Paints appeared in 1962 when an advertising agency for ICI were shooting a TV commercial in which there was a family scene. One of the agency executives thought the room looked too sterile, and that it might look more lived-in if it included a large furry dog. Later, when the agency was conducting routine research into the effectiveness of the advertising, it was noticed that there had been a very high level of recall of the dog, so it was decided to use him in subsequent commercials.

Dash, as the first Dulux dog was called, retired after eight years and was replaced by Digby who was chosen after a national competition. However, Digby was eventually retired and has been replaced.

ICI and their advertising agency have a close relationship with the dogs, and their owners. In addition to the dogs actually used on television, ICI have a team of Dulux dogs which are used at fetes, store openings and charity events. Each dog has to undergo very careful scrutiny to ensure it meets the requirements of appearance, personality and temperament—particularly as the dogs are surrounded by children almost everywhere they go.

Esso

Standard Oil (SO) of New Jersey was originally founded in the late nineteenth century by John D. Rockefeller. It was the chief company of a Trust uniting many oil interests in the United States, but as there were numerous Standard Oil companies, the initials SO caused confusion. By pre-fixing ES to SO the resulting name ESSO remained phonetically the same as before and became the Company's registered trademark, signified by the Esso oval. It is used world-wide except in the United States where, following a court case, it became known by its new registered trademark, EXXON.

In 1911, the Supreme Court had dissolved the original Standard Oil Trust into 34 unrelated units and part of the

Court's decision was that the brand Esso should not be used in those parts of the Union where the newly formed Standard Oil companies were established as a result of the break-up. Esso fought unsuccessfully to establish their right to retain their national trademark, but the Court's judgement maintained that Esso meant Standard Oil to the public. Consequently, Standard Oil of New Jersey, who had inherited the Esso brand Name, were unable to advertise it by this name in certain parts of America. In strictest secrecy the Company searched for a new trademark for use in America. A word was needed that could identify both the company and its services, preferably a word having no actual meaning, nor adverse connotations in English or in any other language; a short word with impact, and easy to remember.

A computer was used. 10,000 names were produced. Hundreds of participants helped in a prolonged opinion research poll until the list was reduced to 234, and then to 6 finalists. Linguistic studies were made on them in more than 100 languages. Nearly 7,000 people were interviewed, including 4,000 people in 40 different cities in the United States.

From this sampling, Exxon was chosen as the new trademark for Esso in America.

4711

It was the closing of the monastries by the French during the Napoleonic Wars that indirectly led to the founding of the firm of '4711'. In 1792, in the prosperous city of Cologne on the banks of the Rhine, a wealthy young banker called Mulhens and his wife-to-be received the apparently simple gift of an ancient scrap of paper. It came from a Carthusian monk, in gratitude for his having been given refuge by the Mulhens family. It was the secret formula for making genuine eau de cologne, *Aqua Mirabilis*, the miracle water, as it was then called. Soon, the astute young banker foresaw its commercial opportunities and began to make his *Aqua Mirabilis* to the secret formula in the family home. It quickly became the favourite purchase of local dignitaries and fashionable women to whom, in those days, the 'sweet-smelling waters' with the magical properties were a virtual necessity.

Two years later, Cologne was again occupied by Napoleon and, because his billeting officer was no doubt confused by so many small streets, on orders of the commanding general each house in the city was numbered consecutively.

The French officers soon discovered the delights of the *Aqua Mirabilis* sold at *numero* 4711 and sent flasks of it home to their wives and sweethearts. The women were delighted, having been deprived of such luxuries since the Revolution. Orders soon poured in to the house in the *Glockengasse* for this wonderful water of Cologne.

The Mulhens family registered the house number as its trademark, only adding a bell to indicate its origin in the *Glockengasse*, Bell Lane.

Glaxo

The name Glaxo for dried, skimmed milk was approved in the early 1900s, but only after the Register of Companies in London had turned down as unacceptable the word Lacto—a previously proposed trademark for the same product. So a further list of similar-sounding names was then submitted, Glaxo among them.

Glaxo, which was to become a world-wide success story to the benefit of mankind, had a modest beginning. In 1873, in Wellington, New Zealand, an English immigrant called Joseph Nathan began importing milk-drying machines. By the early 1900s he was exporting dried, skimmed milk to England.

A large and very successful advertising campaign in 1913 to promote Glaxo Infant Food, included the slogan 'Glaxo Builds Bonny Babies'. This slogan fired the imagination and swept the country, prompting a music-hall-style quip of the time about the young husband who was supposed to have asked: 'Who takes it—me or the wife?'.

Following the success of its baby food sales, the company's operation extended into pharmaceuticals. And later, in 1943, Glaxo Laboratories also entered the antibiotics field as one of the pioneer manufacturers charged with the task of mass-producing penicillin—discovered by Sir Alexander Fleming and developed by Florey, Raistrick and Chain—and acknowledged to be Britain's greatest twentieth-century contribution to medicine.

In 1947 Glaxo Laboratories Limited absorbed its parent company, Joseph Nathan & Company, and began to expand its interests in the United Kingdom. Today, the Glaxo

Group is a leading international group of companies. The Group conducts research and develops, manufactures and markets a wide range of antibiotics, vaccines, vitamins, vetinary products, fine chemicals, foods, surgical instruments, hospital equipment and agricultural and garden chemicals.

Inside almost any hospital, chemist's cupboard, or home medicine chest you will see, somewhere, the name Glaxo.

Guinness

Although Guinness has been brewed in Dublin for well over 200 years, it was on 5 April 1962 that the Harp symbol was registered as a Guinness trademark, and it first appeared on labels on 18 August of that year. The design is based on the O'Neill harp, popularly known as Brian Boru's harp, which has for many years appeared as the principal Irish symbol. The Guinness harp is a reverse portrayal of the 'official' Irish harp.

It is, of course, easy to see the connection that an Irish harp has with a beer which has been brewed in Dublin since 1759, but Arthur Guinness, Son & Company also have another trademark—the toucan first registered in July 1953—an attractive tropical American bird with an immense beak. Why the toucan? Like so many of the best creative ideas, there is no real logic behind the choice. It emerged in 1935 as the brainchild of Dorothy L. Sayers, the novelist, and John Gilroy, the artist, both of whom were working at the time for S. H. Benson, the advertising agency. Apparently it all stemmed from the idea that if one Guinness is good for you, imagine what two can do! Hence the verse used in the first toucan advertisement:

> If he can say as you can
> Guinness is good for you
> How grand to be a toucan
> Just think what two can do.

Harris Tweed

There can be few more distinctive trademarks than that of Harris Tweed. Its special design of an orb surmounted by a Maltese cross was registered in 1909. It is stamped every three yards on the finished cloth by means of a transfer which also states where it was woven. The orb mark is also a prominent feature of the garment label issued by the Harris Tweed Association.

The mark is the exclusive property of the Harris Tweed Association which was formed for the promotion and protection of the Harris Tweed industry. The orb symbol came from the Arms of the Earl of Dunmore in acknowledgement and appreciation of the role played by the Countess of Dunmore in promoting Harris Tweed for the benefit of the islanders in the 1850s. The orb mark certifies that cloth bearing it is genuine Harris Tweed and that it conforms to the definition approved by the Board of Trade—a Tweed made from pure virgin wool produced in Scotland, spun, dyed and finished in the Outer Hebrides and handwoven by the Islanders at their own homes in the Islands of Lewis, Harris, Uist, Barra and their several purtenances and all known as the Outer Hebrides.

Harris Tweed is exported to about 32 countries and the trademark is registered in 26 of them and registrations in 3 more countries have been applied for. Just as the orb is recognised to represent the world, so many people of the world now recognise Harris Tweed.

Heinz

The '57 Varieties' slogan came to Henry Heinz in 1896 while he was travelling through New York City on the overhead railway. He noticed a card in a street-car window advertising shoes—'21 Styles', liked the idea and decided to adapt it for his company. He knew that there were about 60 Heinz varieties on the market but was not sure of the exact number; although he could list as many as 58 or 59, he chose the number 57—it somehow sounded right and appealed to him because of the psychological significance of the numbers 5 and 7.

The new slogan was printed and distributed throughout the USA on the street-car card designed by Henry Heinz himself; he later said 'I myself did not realise how successful a slogan it was going to be'.

Henry John Heinz was born in 1844. At the age of 12 he worked for a neighbouring farmer, picking potatoes for 25 cents a day and meals. Later, he worked in his father's brickyard, but in his spare time he grew and sold garden produce which meant rising at 3am to start the 6-mile wagon trip to Pittsburgh to deliver vegetables. From his profits he was able, in 1869, to found the firm of Heinz and Noble who raised, grated and bottled horseradish. The business continued to grow until the stock market collapsed in 1875 and Henry went bankrupt. He personally charged himself with the responsibility of paying each of his creditors in full; he finally won his discharge from bankruptcy in 1885 and shortly afterwards the company of H. J. Heinz was registered. Today, with its headquarters on Pittsburgh's North Side, it has factories in the United States, Canada, Portugal, Italy, Venezuela, Mexico, Japan, Britain, Australia and Holland. Heinz products are sold in more than 150 countries around the world.

His Master's Voice

How many people have looked at certain music records and wondered about the dog that is depicted with a puzzled expression and head slightly cocked as it listens to a gramophone?

This trademark has had a complicated history. EMI own it in most countries, while RCA own it in North and South America, the Phillipines, Taiwan, Hong Kong and South Korea, and JVC own it in Japan.

Its story started in 1899 when the artist Francis Barraud approached the Gramophone Company to borrow a gramophone. He had painted a picture of a dog listening to a phonograph, but the result was not satisfactory; he preferred to paint the dog listening to the gramophone because the gramophone horn was larger and made of brass, which would give more light to the picture. He borrowed a gramophone, painted out the phonograph, and replaced it with a gramophone.

The idea for the picture originated because Francis Barraud's own dog, Nipper, used to sit like that, listening to the phonograph with that same puzzled expression. Barraud named his finished picture *His Master's Voice*, and the Gramophone Company bought it from him and adopted it as their trademark.

Hoover

So famous has this name become that it is sometimes erroneously used when referring to any make of vacuum cleaner as used in the phrase 'Hoovering the carpet'. But the Hoover trademark in this country belongs exclusively to Hoover Limited. It was registered in the United Kingdom on 9 August 1921 but before then in the United States, and today it is registered in over 100 countries throughout the world.

The name comes from the late Mr W. H. 'Boss' Hoover whose family, in the early 1900s, was known throughout the United States as manufacturers of good quality harness and saddlery. But the inventor of today's 'Hoover' was a relative, Mr Murray J. Spangler.

Murray Spangler suffered from asthma. He worked as a janitor, and the dust from his broom affected his health. He hit on an idea which might help overcome this. In June 1907 he brought a model of his 'electric suction sweeper' to 'Boss' Hoover and his sons. It was a crude machine made of tin and wood, with a broom handle and a sateen bag. But the Hoover family had already recognised that the start of the 'car age' would eliminate the market for saddles and harnesses and were looking around for other possible enterprises. 'Boss' Hoover saw the potential in Spangler's idea. In 1908 he began manufacturing a refined model of the cleaner Spangler had introduced, which was to become known, worldwide, as a Hoover.

Hush Puppies

Since 1958 a sad-eyed basset hound has helped to sell over 158 million Hush Puppies shoes in 54 countries manufactured by Wolverine World Wide, Inc, Rockford, Michigan, USA, and its licensees throughout the world.

Until 1957 the only Hush Puppies that people had ever

heard of were corn fritters which people down in the Southern States threw to their barking dogs with the command 'Hush, puppies'. It seemed appropriate to Wolverine to give this name to a comfortable shoe that was kind to the feet and hushed that special kind of 'barking dog'.

The Company's dedication to developing the art of leather tanning and shoemaking started at the end of the Napoleonic Wars when Valentine Krause returned to his home town in Prussia, Germany, to become a tanner. His son Henry served his apprenticeship in this Old World Tannery, and went to America in 1844. He established a tannery in Michigan, and his skills were passed down to his sons and grandsons.

In the early 1930s, the Wolverine Shoe and Tanning Corporation developed a triple-tanning process for producing suede pigskin leather for work gloves—using surplus bacon rinds of the packing houses which had begun to pre-package sliced bacon.

Later, Wolverine, as tanners of horse-hide leather, found their raw materials diminishing as American farmers began to use tractors, and fewer horses. Because of its earlier success with smoked bacon rinds, Wolverine tried to solve this raw materials shortage with 'green' (unsmoked) pigskins. Pigskin had not been much of a volume leather source in the past; it clings to a pig as apple-skin does to an apple. Wolverine spent seven years and several million dollars inventing a machine to skin the pig—and finally developed the tannage that made this pigskin into the quality shoe leather used for Hush Puppies.

Today, Hush Puppies shoes are made by Wolverine's Hush Puppies Licensee in West Germany, Alfred Malich, about 40 miles from where the founding Krause family started over a century before.

Idem

As this carbonless copying paper, manufactured in South Wales and Belgium, is sold in 75 countries excluding North America, there must be users in most continents who recognise Idem for what it is, and does. For them it means no more forgotten carbons, slipped carbons, or carbons inserted the wrong way up, no interleave sheets to insert and align or smudge. Idem has gone into the language of the office and the world of business. A neat little word that slips off the tongue. 'Pass the Idem.' 'We need more Idem.'

Idem is the Wiggins Teape trademark for carbonless copying paper and was introduced in 1970. The paper, which at that time was produced under license to the National Cash Register Company, used to be called 'NCR paper'.

In 1970, Wiggins Teape changed the name of this carbonless copying paper to Idem—a Latin word meaning 'the same'. This was chosen partly to reflect the fact that the product remained the same, even if the name had changed, and also because the paper is used to produce copies which are exactly the same as each other.

Just as the word 'ditto' is used in Britain, so the word used in many other countries is 'idem'.

Imperial Leather

It came as no surprise to learn that the name Imperial Leather owes its origin to an aristocrat. In the late 1780s a Russian courtier, Count Orlof, visited London's leading perfumiers, Bayley's of Bond Street. Bayley's held Royal warrants from King George III, George IV and William IV, and enjoyed an exclusive clientele including Beau Brummel, Lord Nelson and Lady Hamilton.

Count Orlof commissioned Bayley's to create an entirely new perfume for him, one which would be strongly suggestive of the distinctive aroma of leather. The new fragrance, which was made up of 21 essential oils, was named 'Eau de Cologne Imperial Leather Russe'.

One hundred and fifty years later, Mr. Cussons bought Bayley's of Bond Street and, at about the same time, the Company decided to invest in a Soap Room at Kersal Vale. It was 1938 and Mr Cusson was looking for a unique fragrance for his soap. He recalled Bayley's history of 'Imperial Russe' which, he decided, fitted what he was looking for perfectly. Today the soap is exported to 120 countries.

Isopon

Isopon, registered on 11 October 1956, is another trademark which has a nice sound and looks right. In block letters it identifies a wide range of products from Liquid Rubba to Zinc Anti-rust Coat, from aluminium mesh to repair paste kits for the do-it-yourself man. But Isopon—what does it mean?

Isopon was actually coined from another trademark; one which belonged to Mr Bernhard David, a manufacturing chemist who founded his business in 1908 in Hamburg, Germany, and manufactured chemical products under the trademark Isolament. 'Iso' is derived from the German word *Isolieren* meaning to insulate.

In 1938 Bernhard David's son, Mr Walter David, took refuge in England for political reasons and served six years in the British Army. After his demobilisation, he started his own manufacturing business in an old stable in premises near King's Cross, London, with a capital of £400 (part of which was his Army gratuity). He manufactured polyester bodyfillers for use on a large scale for the repair of dents in motorbodies and, for a trademark for his entirely new product, he used part of his father's trademark, Isolament, to invent Isopon—hoping this would bring him luck.

From the beginning, Mr David concentrated on exports which he knew were so important to the country. He developed his business, without any loans whatsoever, by ploughing back most of the profits.

Although the trademark Isopon was originally intended for polyester bodyfillers, it is now applicable to all car-care and other products manufactured by David's.

Although in his 70s, Mr Walter David is continuing to be very active, ably assisted by his two sons (the third generation). He maintains still that he owes much to England. But today, with exports of David's ISOPON amounting to over two million pounds sterling annually, could it be that England owes something to men like Mr David?

Jaguar

The name 'Jaguar', a registered trademark, originally referred to a specific range of cars from 1935—SS Jaguar 1½, 2½ and 3½ litre saloons and the SS Jaguar 100. This name was chosen by Sir William Lyons from a selection of about 500 names of birds, animals and fish. The animal seemed to suit the character of the cars depicting grace, speed and beauty.

Mr Lyons, as a young motorcycle enthusiast, began his business life in 1922 in partnership with Bill Walmsley. They formed the Swallow Sidecar Company to manufacture sidecars for motorcycles in an old building in Bloomfield Road, Blackpool, England. But by 1927, William Lyons' acute business sense and flair for coach-body design, had found expression in the Swallow-bodied Austin 7. After that, he turned out a succession of cars based on mechanical components made by Standard, but they were so well styled and competitively marketed that the company became known in 1935 as SS Cars Limited. Whether the initials SS stood for Swallow Special, or Standard Swallow, has been argued; Lyons has never said. But by 1945, with memories of World War Two still fresh, the initials SS were more likely to be associated with the *Schützstaffel*, and the name of the company was changed to Jaguar Cars Limited.

In 1961, with the introduction of the E-type, the word Jaguar acquired a new connotation. For many people there was no greater status symbol, nor other car that a girl would prefer to be whisked away in; a 'Jag' became an accepted term in English usage.

Almost as famous as the cars are the badges, emblems, insignia, and the leaping cat which are symbolic of the Jaguar.

Kiwi Polish

The kiwi bird undoubtedly looks neat and attractive, but it is less obvious perhaps that love played a major part in the success of the product which it symbolises. It was in the little seaport of Oamaru on the east coast of South Island, New Zealand, that Annie Elizabeth Meek was born and brought up, and fell in love with William Ramsay, an

Australian. In 1901 they married and went to live in Melbourne. There the attractive, energetic Annie became a housewife, mother, and inspiration to her husband who was laying the foundations of what was to become a gigantic business enterprise.

In 1906, William developed a new shoe polish—naming it Kiwi in honour of his beloved wife's New Zealand origin.

Kiwi happens to be easy to read and pronounce in most languages, which is perhaps why there have been numerous attempts at copying the famous design. They range from identical copies to similar designs with different birds or animals as illustrations, with almost invariably the original layout and colour combination maintained. And (although imitation is said to be the sincerest form of flattery), the Company is constantly engaged in tracing and preventing imitations. So far they have occurred in Finland, India, Vietnam, Singapore, Korea, Japan, Indonesia, Mainland China, Israel, and Egypt. The original Kiwi polish is today sold in 173 countries, and manufactured in 19.

Knorr®

This registered trademark derived its name from Carl Heinrich Knorr who founded the original company in Heilbronn, Germany, in 1838. He traded in cereals and was later joined by his two sons. Eduard Knorr had spent time in France where he had seen the first soup powders made from dried vegetables and seasonings. Both brothers saw the potential and began to experiment. Their first dehydrated product, around 1880, was a 'sausage' made of dried peas; a slice in boiling water made pea soup. Later, they sold a soup tablet weighing 100 grams and costing 15 Pfennig. Eduard was well-known in the streets of Heilbronn for distributing soup cubes from his pockets to passers-by.

In 1885, the company opened packing plants in Austria and Switzerland. Fridtjof Nansen, the Norwegian explorer, took Knorr products on his North Pole Expedition in 1893; British troops used them during the Boer War.

In 1944, an Allied bombing raid destroyed the Heilbronn factory. For some years, the Swiss affiliate took the lead and, in 1956, the Swiss Knorr Company opened a plant in Welwyn Garden City for the British market. By the late 1950s, the Heilbronn plant was re-established, but needed resources for its expansion projects. Although then acquired by an American corn wet-milling company, now CPC International Inc, Knorr today forms an important part of the consumer business of that company—and its trademark remains as it has appeared on letterheads from very early times in distinctive script.

Kosset Carpets

Anyone can see that a certain white cat which disports itself on rich carpets, obviously living the life of Riley, is no common old moggy, nor an artist's impression. So, to whom does it belong? What has it to do with carpets? Does he, or she, answer to a name other than 'Puss'?

This symbol of Kosset Carpets Limited is a pure thoroughbred with a tremendous pedigree, and is affectionately known to the firm by his pet name of Huggy Bear, though his real name is Jerami Michaelson. It was about 25 years ago, when the company was founded, that a white chinchilla cat was first chosen to represent luxury, softness and perfection.

Today's Huggy Bear is a son of a previous Kosset cat which died some years ago. Not surprisingly, the company regards Huggy as a VIP and look after him in a manner befitting his importance.

LEGO®

50 million children all over the world are playing with LEGO bricks. LEGO leaflets are printed in 25 languages so that the world's children will understand them. LEGO is so named everywhere, but why LEGO?

The LEGO story began in the 1930s when Ole Kirk Christiansen, a carpenter in the tiny village of Billund on the moors of Jutland, lost his job because of the Depression in Denmark. He had an idea which he started to realise—to create good toys which would appeal to children's imagination and which would withstand rough handling. He called his toys LEGO.

Christiansen did not know that LEGO, in Latin, means 'I am reading' or 'I am joining together'. He had created the name LEGO by putting together the Danish words *leg godt* meaning 'play well'.

The sturdy wooden toys, yo-yo's, elephants on wheels, and many more, became a success. As business progressed, he employed more craftsmen. It took much thought and many experiments before the LEGO brick as we know it today was introduced on the market in the 1950s. But in consequence of its success, in a few generations, Billund has developed from being only a few farms where the stagecoach stopped occasionally to an address which exports 97% of its production to 106 countries.

To millions of people, playing with LEGO bricks is, or was, part of their childhood. Always LEGO—play well.

Lemon Hart Rum

When I first heard this name, before I had seen it in print, I visualised a tot of rum with an added dash of lemon in the middle, or very heart. I might have learnt a lot more about how widely wrong I was if United Rum Merchants Limited, who market this product, had not been severely bombed in the Mark Lane, Eastcheap, area of the City of London during the Second World War. All records were lost.

But it is known that Lemon Hart (son of Lazarus Hart who died in 1803), was a wine and spirit merchant of Penzance, Cornwall, in the latter part of the eighteenth and the early part of the nineteenth centuries. In those days Penzance was an area notorious for swashbuckling pirates. And as Mr Hart's trade was largely with the West Indies, Penzance in an age of sail was the nearest landfall and a very appropriate venue from which to conduct a rum importing business. It is believed, too, that Hart was the first victualler of rum to the British Navy.

The Hart family was known to be Jewish, and it is assumed that the name Lemon Hart was originally Leahman Hart. After his death in Penzance on 7 October 1845 at the age of 75, others continued trading under an anglicisation of the founder's former name, so that it became Lemon Hart Rum.

Lloyds Bank

In my youth, I was convinced that members of Lloyds Banks were admirers of Anna Sewell, and that *Black Beauty* was their compulsory reading. That is, until I discovered that their black horse symbol is first recorded as appearing in London's Lombard Street, in 1666.

The Sign of the Black Horse hung outside the establishment of Humphrey Stokes, a goldsmith, listed in a London Directory of Merchants published in 1677, but historians believe he inherited the sign from his father, dating it back to the early days of Charles II (1660s), or earlier. Although these London goldsmiths were the forerunners of modern British banking, it was not until after many new partnerships and mergers had taken place that, in 1884, the Black Horse hanging sign logo became Lloyds own symbol. And now, more than 300 years after it was featured on Humphrey Stokes' sign, it hangs in modernised form outside almost every Lloyds branch in England and Wales. It can also be seen in California, Russia and Japan, and is recognised worldwide.

Marmite

There seems to be no record of exactly when, where or by whom this name was adopted. But it is believed to be derived from the small pot of the same name used extensively in France for cooking. And this French association is highly probable, according to the history of the product, and also the entry of its proprietary name in the *Oxford Dictionary*: Marmite. Extract made from fresh brewer's yeast. F. (French) = Cooking-pot.

It was, after all, the French scientist Pasteur who, with the German chemist Liebig, developed the idea of producing yeast extract. Until the result of their brilliant research work in the second half of the nineteenth century, although yeast had been known to ancient civilisations, its use had been unrecognised, dismissed as a mere useless by-product.

After several attempts on the continent to make such an

extract, Marmite was first manufactured in England in 1902. Since then, the process has been developed further to produce an improved yeast extract flavoured with vegetable extracts, a dietary source of all the B-complex vitamins, particularly useful in Malaya, Africa, India and other countries where people suffer from malnutrition.

Maxwell House Coffee

It was through a fine hotel that this coffee came by its name, a coffee story which began in 1873 when 21-year-old Joel Cheek left his family farm in Kentucky to seek his fortune. He joined a wholesale grocery firm as a travelling salesman and acquired a peculiar fascination for coffee. He spent his spare time experimenting with different types of coffee beans. In 1882 he set up in business on his own and devoted all his time to the search for a perfect blend of coffee. When he thought he had achieved his objective, he was anxious to try it out on some really discerning palates. He went to what was probably the finest hotel in the Southern States and a favourite meeting place for presidents, generals, diplomats and European nobility—the Maxwell House at Nashville.

The management of Maxwell House gave Cheek's new blend a trial and, within weeks, the new coffee was a success with the hotel's guests. Theodore Roosevelt's reported remark in its favour created an advertising slogan which the company still uses, 'good to the last drop'. In 1929, Cheek's Company (by now, Cheek-Neal Company, coffee roasters and blenders), joined with General Foods Corporation who, in the early 1930s began research into possible techniques for making 'instant' coffee. By 1942 the first shipments of instant coffee were despatched to US forces overseas.

The Maxwell House Hotel was for many years preserved as a fine example of nineteenth-century design and architecture but in 1961 it was burned to the ground, leaving behind only its name as a household synonym for coffee.

Michelin
(Bibendum—the Michelin Man)

It was an innocent remark that was to create this trademark. At the Lyons Exhibition in 1898, brothers André and Edouard Michelin, inventors of these tyres, found that their stand manager had stacked the tyres in assorted sizes in order to try to present them in a novel way. 'Look André,' said Edouard, pointing to one of the stacks of tyres, 'if it had arms it would look like a man.'

André recalled this incident when, some while later, he was visited by a Monsieur O'Galop and shown some sketches for advertisements. André caught sight of a cartoon which O'Galop had just received from a German beer manufacturer. It portrayed a rotund gentleman raising his beer mug and announcing 'Nunc est Bibendum'—'Now is the time to drink'. André told O'Galop of Edouard's imaginative observation at the Exhibition and the artist got to work. The tyre-man replaced the robust drinker; the beer mug was replaced by a champagne glass full of nails and broken glass. Even 'Nunc est Bibendum' was related to the slogan that had become the Michelin motto 'Tyres swallow obstacles'—and the Michelin man was born. But still nameless, he was finally christened at the 1898 Paris-Amsterdam race by the racing driver Thery who, on seeing André Michelin go by, called out 'Look, there is Bibendum'. The Michelin Company accepted the name with delight; it summed up the tyre-man in one word.

Bibendum caught the imagination of the artists. Soon Bibendum appeared with legs. With the stroke of a pen he walked, danced, jumped and ran. He laughed, cried, became angry, pensive, tender. Given the necessary equipment, he undertook any task.

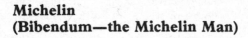

Midland Bank

This griffin, a fabulous creature with an eagle's head and wings, and a lion's body, portrayed within a circlet of bezants, has been the house symbol of Midland Bank since

July 1965. It is a stylised version of the badge which had been authorised as part of the armorial bearings granted to the Bank by the King of Arms in 1952, which was 'within a circlet of bezants a griffin segreant Or'. The griffin was a traditional guardian of treasure, the bezants were gold coins. This house symbol is used on all official publications and displays as well as on Midland Bank premises.

The Bank was founded in Birmingham as the Birmingham and Midland Bank in 1836. In 1891 the Head Office moved to London, and it became the London and Midland Bank. Largely by absorbing other banks including the City Bank and uniting them into one organisation, a branch system was established providing a countrywide banking service. The Bank's present title was adopted in 1923.

The Mouse
(Trademark of a Master Carver)

It is impossible to name all the abbeys, cathedrals, churches, colleges, libraries, schools, stately and even humble homes in which the craftsmanship of Robert Thompson is symbolised by a mouse hand-carved in English oak. The mouse decorates countless font-covers, altar rails, lecterns, pews, organ screens, reredos and candlesticks. It embellishes Church and domestic furniture and very much more, in places as wide apart as North Wales and Sussex; Lustleigh in Devonshire and Inverness, the Outer Hebrides and the Isle of Skye; from York Minster to London's Westminster Abbey.

But why a Mouse?

It is recorded that Thompson was carving a huge cornice for a screen when Charlie Barker, another carver who was helping him, said something about their being as poor as church mice. It is not known if Thompson was looking for a trademark, but he carved a mouse there and then. Relating the incident, he likened the mouse to himself as being industrious in quiet places, and said: 'So I put the mouse on all my work'.

Robert Thompson was born on 7 May 1876, in Kilburn, Yorkshire, son of a village carpenter. At the age of 20, after serving five unhappy years apprenticed to a firm of engineers at Cleckheaton, he joined his father in his carpenter's workshop. On his route between Cleckheaton and Kilburn, he had often visited Ripon Cathedral and been inspired by the carvings of William Bromflet. Subsequently, Thompson formed what was to become a lifelong passion for hand-carving in English oak. He said: 'My work will last 1000 years'.

In 1928, Thompson's order from America for a dining table and four chairs was the first of the 'mouse's' introductions to almost all quarters of the globe. Four mice embellish the South African espiscopal home of the bishop of Natal, The Rt. Rev. T. G. V. Inman. Many carvings went to Australia; an envelope sent from there with merely the picture of a mouse and the words 'Wood Carver, Yorkshire' arrived in Kilburn without delay.

National Benzole

Mr Mercury must surely be the only trademark to have inspired a fashion in ladies' hats! But when National Benzole's 'Mercury Head' logo, with its dashing winged headgear was first to be seen everywhere, it became a popular subject with Bright Young Things at fancy dress dances. (Though it is not recorded whether National Benzole's striking idea of portraying the entire Mr Mercury with athletic, bronzed and startlingly naked body bounding across the pages of the national dailies in 1928 inspired similar results).

National Benzole was founded in 1919, in Horseferry Road, London. As a marketing company, its job was to sell. Benzole, a by-product of coal, had been produced to excess by the end of the First World War and a huge marketing effort was needed to use the excess capacity that had been created.

In the 1920s, the company extolled the virtues of the new motor spirit with a good deal of play on the word 'Spirit'. 'The Spirit of the Future', 'That's the Spirit', and so on, though 'The Spirit with the Devil in it' had to be dropped when it caused a storm among certain religious bodies.

During this time, National Benzole was constantly searching for a suitable trademark. For a while, the jocular Old King Cole was featured in advertisements to remind motorists of benzole's carboniferous origin. But this approach was finally dropped in 1928 in favour of the ideal and recognised association between Mercury—the winged, fleet-footed, Jack-of-all-Trades Roman God—and the all-round 'Power with Economy' of National Benzole Mixture.

The original 'Mercury Head' logo was obviously derived from an idea and grew—or rather was reduced—from the whole body. In 1959, the old logo was redesigned as the centrepiece of a new-look network décor, marking the Company's fortieth anniversary. Today, with a slight rounding-off of the lettering and the corners, that same (1959) distinctive design of the 'Mercury Head' logo with the eye-catching new blue and yellow livery can still be widely seen and recognised as the trademark of National Benzole.

Nestlé's Milk

Birds in a nest—the Nestlé's trademark—was designed by Henri Nestlé who founded the company in Vevey, Switzerland, in 1866. Henri Nestlé, a research chemist, regarded the nest as his coat of arms as well as a trademark—Nestlé means 'little nest' in the German dialect of Switzerland.

Although their milk products, found throughout the world, have differing local brand names, the name Nestlé's appears on every tin as a guarantee of quality.

The original idea for condensed milk was Napoleon's. He asked his scientists to experiment with the preservation of milk in a concentrated form to nourish his soldiers, and to simplify feeding them on the march, but these experiments were not very successful. Eventually, it was American influence which contributed to the successful history of condensed milk. In 1867, the United States Consul in Zurich, Charles Page, founded the Anglo-Swiss Condensed Milk Company. His amalgamation in 1905 with Henri Nestlé, who had invented and developed a milk food for feeding babies, was really the beginning of the Nestlé organisation that has made Nestlé's a household word in many countries.

The Observer

The *Observer* has, of course, used many emblems other than the coat-of-arms with 'Established 1791' printed below, that appears today on the top left- and right-hand corners of its front page. The first issue of the paper on Sunday, 4 December, 1791, showed the sunburst with central eye with the words 'Sunday Advertiser' below; the only available explanation for its use seems to be that it was intended to represent the dawn of a new era.

As for the coat-of-arms used today which is similar to the Royal coat-of-arms but has several differences, the most probable explanation is that it implies support for the principle of the Monarchy—without necessarily implying approval of a particular Monarch, for example, George IV. It indicates that the newspaper in question was not republican in its sympathies. Such an indication must obviously have had the approval of the newspaper's owners when the emblem was first shown.

Olympic Games

The symbol of five linked rings, coloured blue, black, red, yellow and green respectively, was introduced in 1906. The rings represent the five continents joined to symbolise fraternity and friendship, and the symbol was adopted for the Olympic flag design in 1913 at the instigation of Baron Pierre de Coubertin. The first actual flag was hoisted at the 7th International Olympic Games held in 1920 at Antwerp. The City Corporation presented a flag to the International Olympic Committee, which has since been passed from Games to Games, though, of course, replicas are widely used.

The Olympic Games, in their modern form, date only from 1896 when they were held in Athens on the initiative of Baron Pierre de Coubertin, but they may be regarded as the parallel of the Olympic Games of the ancient Greeks which date back to 776BC, and were abolished about AD 393 by the Emperor Theodosius I. For more than a thousand years, the Games of the ancient Greeks took place every four years in high summer at the time of the full moon in honour of Zeus, the supreme god of the Greeks.

In the fifth-century BC the festival lasted for five days. On the first day the athletes' oaths were taken in the *Bouleuterion* (council house) and they were scrutinised to determine their eligibility. On the second day the horse and chariot races took place, and the pentathlon (a competition in five events of running, jumping, throwing the discus and the javelin, and wrestling). The fifth day saw the celebration and prizes—simple wreaths from a sacred olive tree planted, according to tradition, by Hercules, the founder of the Games. The crowned winners marched in procession and triumphant songs were chanted.

Today, at the close of each Olympiad when the trumpet sounds, the fire is extinguished and the Olympic flag is lowered; there is a salute of five guns and the final anthem is sung. Throughout the symbolic number five is repeated—as featured in the Olympic Games symbol.

Oscar

Oscar, the golden symbol of fame presented by the Academy of Motion Picture Arts and Sciences, is fully protected by copyright, and is produced by only one manufacturer, licensed by the Academy. He is ten inches high, weighs seven pounds, his insides being bronze and his exterior gold plate.

But why the name Oscar?

Oscar was nameless when he came into the world as an award symbol in 1927, the year the Academy was founded. For the next four years he was referred to as 'the statuette'. The idea for a statuette originated at a meeting of the first board of governors of the Academy. The executive art director for Metro-Goldwyn-Mayer, Cedric Gibbons, after hearing various suggestions, urged that the awards should be represented by a figure of individual character and dignity which recipients would be proud to display. He sketched a figure and design as he talked. The drawing was adopted and sent to George Stanley, a Los Angeles sculptor, for execution in the round. From his craftsmanship came the statuette.

In 1931, on a day that Mrs Margaret Herrick (later to become executive secretary of the Academy) reported for her first day's work as librarian, a copy of the statuette stood on an executive's desk. She was formally introduced to it as the foremost member of the organisation. She looked at it for a moment, before saying: 'He reminds me of my Uncle Oscar'.

A newspaper columnist sat nearby. The following day his syndicated copy contained the line: 'Employees have affectionately dubbed their famous statuette 'Oscar'. He has been Oscar ever since.

Ovaltine

Because of the difficulty in registering the trademark 'Ovomaltine' in the United Kingdom prior to the First World War, the name was changed to 'Ovaltine', though the product which is manufactured and supplied from Berne in Switzerland today is still known as Ovomaltine. The name Ovomaltine originated from ovo—egg and of course malt, egg and malt being the basic ingredients of the Ovaltine formula.

More than 100 years ago a Swiss chemist, Dr George Wander, set up a laboratory in Berne to investigate the nutritional value of barley malt. The qualities proved so impressive he commenced manufacture of malt extract which culminated in 1904 with the launching of a product to become known all over the world as Ovomaltine or Ovaltine.

At first, in 1909, when the company was founded in the United Kingdom, Ovaltine was shipped in bulk from Switzerland. But four years later a small factory was opened at King's Langley, Hertfordshire. The company expanded during the 1920s and set up its own farm of approximately 460 acres to produce the milk and eggs needed for the manufacture of Ovaltine.

In 1935, the Ovaltiney Club, sponsored by the company, was launched on Radio Luxembourg. This 'secret society' for children with its own badges, rule books, secret codes and comics had, by 1939, five million active club members. 'We are the Ovaltineys' became one of the most evocative jingles of all time.

The Ovaltine dairy maid has appeared on the tin for over 50 years, but within the last five years Wander Foods, as the company is now known, having extended its knowledge to other products, has used the Wander Foods logo incorporating the dairy maid and the words 'Home of Good Health'. But the large word which still dominates the egg-shape design of the complete label remains Ovaltine.

Penguin Books

As Penguin books were the original paperback publishers, for many years paperback books were called 'Penguins' whether they were published by Penguin Books, or not.

But why a Penguin, anyway?

There seems to have been no authoritative statement about this choice. In 1935 Allen Lane, wishing to set up a paperback reprint house of good books at reasonable prices, decided the format and colour (bright orange) but was unresolved as to what to call them. His secretary is supposed to have said: 'Why not Penguins?'. He thought this a splendid idea, and sent his office boy off to get one drawn. The penguin was devised by Edward Young.

Two years later, Allen Lane was standing by a mainline station bookstall when he heard someone ask for a Pelican book, and he was so alarmed at the prospect of a close rival of that name that he decided to issue Pelicans himself. Thereafter came Puffins, and then Peregrine and Peacock books.

When Penguin Books merged with Longmans in 1970, it assumed responsibility for Longman Young Books, and it was decided to rename them with a bird's name though not beginning with the letter 'P' because they were not paperback. So began Kestrels.

Pepsi-Cola

In 1898, appreciative customers called it 'Brad's drink', as they gathered round the soda fountain in the little drugstore in New Bern, North Carolina. But its creator behind the counter, Caleb D. Bradham, named and registered his new beverage as Pepsi-Cola, a name which was to spread from that little drugstore on the corner of Middle and Pollock Streets to a headquarters in New York, and within 50 years to be sold on franchise throughout the world.

Caleb D. Bradham was born in Chinquapin, North Carolina, in 1867, of aristocratic early American background. He hoped to become a doctor but, after two years at Medical School, his father's business failed and Brad set out to earn his own living. He taught in a New Bern school but, when a local drugstore came on the market he felt, with his medical education, he could become a pharmacist. He had no money and bought the drugstore almost wholly on credit. Across its plate-glass window he proudly put the name Bradham's Pharmacy. He dispensed prescriptions—but when his many customers crowded round the soda fountain which flourished in those days in drugstores and was the equivalent of today's coffee bar, a place to socialise, Bradham being a popular and gregarious man liked to 'tend bar' himself. He began experimenting with new flavour combinations, and came up with what he called Pepsi-Cola.

Today, at the corner of Middle and Pollock Streets, the little drugstore has been replaced by a tall office building but on its roof is, appropriately, a sign—Pepsi-Cola.

Pifco

The word Pifco when seen on hand hair-dryers and bedside lamps, etc, often raises the question—why Pifco?

Pifco is a registered trademark in the United Kingdom and overseas. The name is formed from the initials of the Company—Provincial Incandescent Fittings COmpany—as it was known when it was founded in 1900.

The founder, Mr Joseph Webber (grandfather of the present managing director), opened his first shop, a small lock-up at a rent of ten shillings and sixpence per week, on a ground floor in Corporation Street, Manchester. He sold gas mantles, globes, burners and other accessories which, at that time, was a comparatively new business in Manchester.

As electricity took over from gas as a source of power, the company continued to expand by manufacturing and marketing small electrical appliances and a range of battery-operated products and hand lanterns.

One of the earliest visiting cards used by representatives in the early 1900s depicts a portly gentleman in top hat, double-breasted waistcoat, breeches and high boots. He holds above his head a lighted lamp and, in his other hand, a leaflet marked 'Reduce your GAS BILL'. It was an impressive card. Apart from further pictorial design, there was also listed three registered trademarks owned by the company, Jepco, Pifco and Ohat.

Mr Webber directed the company through fifty years of

steady development and in 1949 the company name, in line with its trademark, was changed to Pifco.

Players Please

Many people have argued about the origins of the strong-featured British seaman portrayed within the frame of a lifebelt with the words PLAYERS PLEASE. Thomas Wood, W. J. Mallone, and others have all claimed to be the original sailor. But in fact he was a figment of an artist's imagination and never existed as a real person.

In 1883, John Player saw the painting at W. J. Parkins & Company of Chester who were using it to advertise their 'Jack's Glory' Cut Cavendish tobacco. He immediately bought it and registered it as a trademark. It is believed that the original painting of this sailor's head was produced by a man named Wright from the Clapham area of London in the mid-nineteenth century. Although entirely imaginary, the picture in its original form could well have been thought a reasonable self-portrait by hundreds of British tars.

In 1888, the lifebelt was added and a final definitive format, very close to the original with the head facing right, was adopted in 1891.

This trademark has been amended from time to time with alterations to the background, collar and cap tally—*Hero*, *Invincible*, *Excellent*, and so on. In 1927 the famous artist Arthur David McCormick was commissioned to produce the final portrait.

The name *Invincible* was dropped after the loss of the vessel of that name at Jutland to avoid giving offence to relatives of those killed in action. *Excellent* was adopted as being the name of the shore-based Gunnery School at Whale Island and, therefore, unsinkable. But it is the sailor from *Hero* that today symbolises Players Please.

Quaker Oats

A Mr Henry Seymour, searching the encyclopaedia for a name to use in incorporating a new oats company, became interested in an article on the Quakers. The purity of the lives of the people, their honesty, strength and manliness, impressed him. Then the parallel between these characteristics and what was needed in character and principle in a new business caught his imagination. So the name 'Quaker' was adopted.

The enterprise had started in 1850 when John Stuart left Scotland for Canada where he bought an old oat mill which produced 25 barrels daily. Years later, he and his son moved to Cedar Rapids, Iowa, where they built a new mill. Today, the Cedar Rapids Mill is the world's largest. Quaker is a worldwide organisation with companies in Australia, Argentina, Brazil, Canada, Columbia, Denmark, France, Holland, Italy, Mexico, Venezuela and the United Kingdom. There are 34 manufacturing plants in the USA alone, with an additional 28 plants in 12 other countries employing 25,000 people.

Quaker's main activities now include cereals, pet foods, pasta, biscuits, confectionery, spreads, mixes, frozen foods, restaurants, speciality chemicals, toys and leisure craft products. The company is still very much a family business; the president of the company is Mr Robert D. Stuart, Jnr, a direct descendant of the original John Stuart of Scotland.

Rentokil

This trademark might reasonably have been called 'Entokil'—the Greek *entos* meaning within, hence entoparasite.

In the early 1920s Westminster Great Hall was infested with deathwatch beetles and the Minister of Works, Sir Frank Baines, asked Harold Maxwell-Lefroy, Professor of Entomology at Imperial College, London, to study ways of exterminating the pests. The Professor worked out various formulations. By 1924, with the help of a Miss Elizabeth Eades, he was sending out bottles of his woodworm fluids from a small factory in Hatton Garden to people who had heard about his work. These bottles contained what he called 'Entokil' fluids.

Tragically, in 1925, Lefroy was accidentally killed by poisonous fumes in a laboratory accident. The following year, the head of the company that had made up the fluids also died. The business would have been wound up but for the remarkable qualities of Miss Eades. She offered to take over the business herself. As Governing Director she set about selling woodworm eradication to antique dealers and architects. The name Entokil was too close to another trademark, so an 'R' was added. Perhaps this was an appropriate letter—Rentokil started with biological pest control against rats.

Today Rentokil, an international organisation concerned with pest control, property protection and wood preservation, is made up of many divisions. In 1965, a milestone in the German company's development was the announcement that Rentokil had obtained a contract to clear the rats out of Hamelin! (Whatever happened to the Pied Piper?)

Robertson's Golden Shred

It was about 1910 that a Robertson Company director first came upon the 'Golly' when visiting America, and thought it would make an appealing mascot and trademark for Robertson's Golden Shred marmalade, and preserves. Almost ever since, the Golly symbol with his red trousers, yellow waistcoat and blue, long-tailed jacket has appeared on every label bearing the Robertson name.

The Golly is said to have been created in America in the late nineteenth-century, one of a series of soft dolls much loved by American children. The most celebrated of these cuddly toys was the Teddy Bear, named after President Theodore Roosevelt.

In 1930 the first enamel brooches were issued featuring six different fruits; each brooch with a Golly's head included as part of its design. Later, the Jolly Golly Mascot appeared and continued until the Second World War but from then on the metal used to make these brooches was needed for the British war effort. But by 1946 the Golly was back again. Since then Golly brooches have appeared in many forms from cricketers with county names, footballers and musicians, to the Golly Lollipop Man which also appears on all the Robertson road safety materials produced for school children.

Only very minor changes have taken place to the actual Golly over the years, the positioning of the eyes, the smoothing of the hair, and updating of the logo. The Golly remains symbolic of every Robertson product.

Rolls-Royce

As far as the Company knows, its symbol was first used in 1906. Its origins are unknown but certainly the name ROLLS-ROYCE, the initials RR together with the mascot fitted on the car's clasic square radiator—'The Spirit of Ecstasy' designed in 1911 by Charles Sykes after being commissioned by Rolls-Royce Ltd, are amongst the world's most famous trademarks.

Charles Stewart Rolls was born in 1877, son of Baron Llangattock. Educated at Eton and Cambridge, he became a speed cyclist for Cambridge which, in those days, was the recognised first step into motoring and aeronautics. He bought a 3¾hp Peugeot—the first car ever seen in Cambridge. In 1902 he started business in Earl's Court selling continental cars to the aristocracy. The following year with a partner, Claude Johnson, he founded C. S. Rolls & Company.

In 1900, Rolls had won the British Thousand Miles Trial in a 12hp Panhard competing against Henry Edmunds—the man who later was to introduce him to Henry Royce.

Frederick Henry Royce was born in 1863 near Peterborough, the son of a miller who five years later moved his family to London. There the young Royce sold newspapers for W. H. Smith at Clapham Junction before becoming a telegraph boy in Mayfair. Later, he served a part apprenticeship to the Great Northern Railway and various electrical firms before setting up his own business, Royce Limited, and becoming, by 1900, a successful manufacturer of electric motors and cranes.

In 1903 he bought a sound 10hp Decauville car made by railway locomotive engineers, but he was confident he could produce better. The following year Henry Edmunds, who had competed with Charles Rolls in the 1900 British Thousand Miles Trial and was now a shareholder in Royce Limited, saw the potential in Royce's little car in production. He wrote to the Hon Charles Rolls suggesting he should see the Royce car. As a result, in May 1904 Rolls and Royce, each a perfectionist in his own field, met at the Midland Hotel, Manchester.

An agreement was made to produce a vehicle using a trademark combining the names of ROLLS as a world-famous speed driver, and ROYCE as the dedicated designer—the Rolls-Royce motor car.

Rothmans of Pall Mall

It is clear why the Rothmans Crest (with its little gold crown), is a fitting trademark for these cigarettes when one learns a little of the history of Rothman's, just as it is equally clear that the trading style 'Rothmans of Pall Mall' and the brand name Pall Mall were chosen because of the geographical location of Rothman's shops.

But the founder of the business did not start with a shop in an exclusive street, patronised by Royalty. Mr Louis Rothman was born in the Ukraine in 1869. He served an apprenticeship with his family who owned a large tobacco factory. In 1887, he arrived in London, worked for three years in the British tobacco industry and, in 1890 with a capital of only £40, started his own business. He acquired the lease of 55a Fleet Street—a mere kiosk, regarded as one of the smallest shops in London. He made cigarettes by night and canvassed sales to Fleet Street newspapermen by day.

In time he was supplying press tycoons such as Lord Rothermere, Sir Arthur Pearson and Lord Northcliffe. He opened additional shops close to the Stock Exchange and, in 1900 a further shop under the famous Carlton Hotel at 5a Pall Mall. This was the centre of London's fashionable clubland and the meeting place of the aristocracy.

In 1905 the King's secretary, Lord Stamfordham, asked Rothman to supply cigarettes to Buckingham Palace and the Royal Yacht. By 1910, Prince Maurice Alexander of Battenburg and King Alfonso XIII of Spain were among his customers. Little need to look further to explain the little gold crown that appears on each cigarette.

St Ivel

What is the connection between cream and lactic cheese and its trademark, St Ivel. Who was this Saint?

Around the turn of the century Mr Barrett, a director of Aplin & Barrett, manufacturers of cheese in England's

47

Westcountry, decided he needed an advertising gimmick. He wove a fictional story about some monks who lived near the River Yeo in Somerset, and who had recipes for a number of table delicacies. Mr Barrett chose Saint Ivel from the River Yeo's Saxon name which was Yivel, Ivel or Gissel. The word lactic (of milk) he took from a culture which is now a common feature of yogurt, *lacto vacillus bulgaris*, named after the Bulgars who consumed large quantities of it in fermented milk and had a reputation for long life and fertility At first the firm claimed these therapeutic properties for its lactic cheese, but later were happy to call it no more than a medium-fat soft cheese. Although produced in the Westcountry, St Ivel became a nationally distributed brand, much respected and sent out to the British troops in the Second World War. So St Ivel cheese, nationally recognised, is named after the old monk who never existed!

St Michael

St Michael

The trademark 'St Michael' was registered on 5 November, 1928. The name was chosen by Simon Marks, son of Michael Marks who founded the firm of Marks and Spencer in 1894. Today it is registered in over fifty countries.

Michael Marks was born in 1863 at Bialystok in what was then Russian Poland. The hardships he shared with the majority of Polish Jews bred in him a sympathetic understanding of the needs of the working classes, particularly of his fellow Jews. When Tsar Alexander II was assassinated, the fresh outbreak of anti-Semitism and persecution it provoked caused a wave of emigration of the Jews.

Michael Marks, a 19-year-old Polish refugee, arrived in England knowing no English, unable to read or write, with no capital, and not trained in any trade. He was a small man, not physically strong, but with a sensitive, kindly nature. By 1884 he had set up business as a pedlar, walking the villages round Leeds carrying his stock on his back.

One of his first suppliers was I. J. Dewhirst Ltd where the cashier, Thomas Spencer, was impressed by the business Michael Marks was doing. That same year, Michael opened a stall in the open market at Kirkgate in Leeds—a 4ft by 6ft trestle table. Later, he moved to the covered market. He classified his goods according to price;

a board hung over the penny section with the slogan: 'Don't ask the price; it's a penny'. He never kept any accounts, but conducted his business operations by mental arithmetic. Soon he was operating five Penny Bazaars. In 1894 he offered Thomas Spencer a half share in the business, and on 28 September, 1894, the firm of Marks and Spencer was formed.

The first firm with which Marks and Spencer were able to establish a direct relationship was the hosiery firm of Messrs Corah near St Margarets Church, Leicester, and which provided Corah with the brand name St Margaret. Marks and Spencer considered a number of Saint's names to go along with St Margaret when, in 1928, they registered their own brand names for goods manufactured to their orders. It was fitting that Simon Mark's choice was St Michael; apart from his father's first name being Michael, the archangel Michael was the guardian angel and patron of the Jewish people.

Shell

The idea for the Shell trademark was taken from the days when Marcus Samuel (born 1853) owned a small business in Houndsditch, trading mainly in importing and selling painted shells. At that time, in England, shells were as valuable as precious stones and widely used in making jewellery and other ornaments. But Marcus Samuel also shipped merchandise such as rice and curios from the East. He became interested in the petroleum industry when he visited Japan, and began shipping oil from Russia to the far East. In 1892, he gave a shell name to his tanker—the *Murex*.

In those days, steamers had to return empty after carrying freight, as it was impossible to clean the holds properly. Eventually, Marcus Samuel worked out how holds could be thoroughly cleaned out by steam, so that ships could be loaded with rice and other Eastern produce for the return journey. This achievement led to his combining with other traders and, backed by the Rothschilds, he founded the Shell Transport and Trading Company in 1897, using the word 'Shell' after his original business.

The first 'shell' registered, a mussel, did not catch on and was changed, in 1904, to a scallop. Since then the Shell trademark has undergone five distinct changes. Like all good trade names it is distinctive, brief, easy to remember and pronounce.

Today, the pecten sign and the word SHELL in the name of a company or on a product are evidence of the worldwide activities of the group of companies.

Spar

A little fir tree within a matching green circlet and the word Spar (denoting a voluntary chain or group of retail and wholesale grocers) can be seen almost anywhere in Europe as well as in South Africa, Greece and Japan.

Just why a fir tree was adopted as the group symbol, and the word 'Spar' as the group name, is easily explained. It was in 1932, in Holland, that the first 'Spar' group trading took place, set up by a Mr A. J. M. van Well, a wholesaler in the Hague. The fir tree—for which the Dutch word is *spar*—was his company's trademark. The Dutch word for savings is *sparen*.

In 1947, the Spar Central Office in the Netherlands was approached by a number of wholesale grocers in Belgium for guidance on forming voluntary groups and, with its help, Spar was launched in Belgium in 1948. During the following years, until 1977, 14 other countries followed. There are nearly 4,000 stores in Spar UK.

In order to co-ordinate the developments in different countries, an international office called Internationale Spar Centrale NV was set up in Amsterdam in 1954.

In 1966, Internationale Spar decided that all parts of the organisation should be identified by a common symbol and commissioned a firm of design consultants in Paris called Compagnie de l'Esthetique Industrielle. Strict design disciplines for its use were laid down, to which all countries voluntarily subscribe.

State Express 555

This rather romantic-sounding name may well conjure up visions of speed, or the title of an Agatha Christie novel; these cigarettes were indeed named after an express train.

In 1895 when Sir Albert Levy, founder of the Ardath Tobacco Company Limited, decided to register the cigarettes he manufactured, he took the name for them from what was then the world's fastest train. The Empire State Express, owned by the New York Central and Hudson River Railroad Company, ran from Buffalo to New York City. And when Sir Albert travelled on the Empire State Express, the engine number was 999. This inspired him to register the numbered combinations 111, 222, 333 and so on up to 999, to be used in association with State Express cigarettes.

In 1925, the Ardath Company was jointly acquired by British-American Tobacco Limited (BAT) and Imperial Tobacco and, in accordance with existing trademark agreements between these companies, BAT took over Ardath's brand sales overseas. Subsequently, BAT exported State Express 555 to China and, because the number five is especially lucky to the Chinese, the success of the cigarettes in that country at that time was in part due to their name—State Express 555.

Swan Vestas

Surely an ideal combination for the name of a match. Swan, the royal bird, and Vesta, the goddess of the hearth whose fire burns perpetually. A trademark so fondly familiar today that it caused the comedian Ken Dodd to quip: 'Stratford-upon-Avon—famous for its swans who pose on matchbox covers'.

The Swan story began in 1883 when Collard & Company of Liverpool, introduced a new match called Swan. The Diamond Match Company of America took over Collard's and, while continuing to manufacture Swan, introduced a different match in 1897 called Swan White Pine Vestas. In 1901, Bryant & May amalgamated with the Diamond Match Company and five years later the words 'White Pine' were dropped from the latest matches.

Many people between 1914-17 never went on a journey

without a box of Swan Vestas, for inside every box, inserted as a ticket, was a free Insurance Policy for £100-£500. One of the conditions for this unique insurance was that a box of Swan Vestas must be on the person at the time of the accident, and that the death must be due to an injury received while travelling.

During the Second World War, contributions from employees of Bryant & May and overseas subsidiaries purchased a Spitfire aptly christened *The Swan* for the RAF. The fighter took part in the historic Battle of Britain.

The captions on the Swan Vestas matchboxes have changed occasionally to meet varying situations: Support Home Industries (1905) The Smoker's Match (1905), Use Matches Sparingly (1941). And, in 1959, the direction in which the swan travels across the box was reversed. But the trademark Swan Vestas remains unchanged.

Texaco

How many people, waiting in their cars at garages, have contemplated the origin of the name Texaco?

Texaco, a registered trademark, originated in the cable address of the Texas Company, founded in the United States in 1902. After it had become established as a brand name, the identification was strengthened in 1959 by changing the corporate name to Texaco Incorporated. In Britain, the trademark came into general use after the Regent Oil Company Limited changed its name to Texaco Limited in 1967, following a change in ownership.

Two versions of the trademark exist. Both have in common the distinctive hexagonal shape in red surrounding the name TEXACO in block capital letters. This is the version used in the United Kingdom and Europe, as well as certain other territories. Another version of the trademark incorporates the letter T on a star, and is used by Texaco Incorporated in the United States and in many other countries. Both are fully protected against infringement.

The Texaco group is involved in exploration, production, refining, transport and marketing activities in most countries of the world.

THERMOS

It is unlikely that the adjudicators of a competition, held in the early 1900s, could have foreseen the sequel to their decision.

The competition was held to find a suitable name for the domestic vacuum flask which had recently been developed in Germany by Reinhold Burger. The prizewinner was a resident of Munich who submitted the name 'Thermos' derived from the Greek word *therme* meaning heat.

In 1907, a few far-sighted English businessmen secured the patent rights for the British Empire, South America and many other countries. They formed the company Thermos Limited and registered the word Thermos as a trademark. It is the sole property of the company wherever it owns the registration and may not be legally applied in these territories to any vacuum vessel not marked with this name. So popular was this invention with its easy-to-say trade name that THERMOS is almost a household word for any vacuum flask. In fact, THERMOS has become so universally accepted that it is to be found in the *Concise Oxford Dictionary*, one of the very few products of a commercial firm to do so.

Three Candlesticks

One might be forgiven for thinking that this high-quality writing paper, produced by John Dickinson's, was probably only called 'Three Candlesticks' because their very appearance conveys such distinction. But there is a deeper reason.

During the seventeenth century in England there was an acute shortage of coins of low denominations. To overcome the difficulties this caused, many traders and municipalities minted and issued farthing and halfpenny tokens made to their own designs. They gave these to their customers as small change for their purchases and promised, ultimately, to redeem them for silver. One such token was discovered in 1799 on the site of John Dickinson's Old Bailey office. About the size of a farthing, the coin has on one side 'At the 3 Candlesticks' and on the other 'In the Ould Baly 1649' and the letters A. I. K.

Although John Dickinson's Old Bailey office was destroyed in the London blitz on the night of 10 May 1941, the token coin found in 1799 has been adopted as the Three Candlesticks watermark. Just as fine papermaking is one of the oldest arts of civilisation, so from history has come the name—Three Candlesticks.

The Times

The attractive clock device which heads its leader page is symbolic of *The Times* newspaper. On one side of the clock against a background of oakleaves and acorns is shown an open book with the words TIMES PAST. On the other side are young leaves, and a scythe in the pages of a closed book marked FUTURE. In the centre, a larger, open book, marked THE TIMES, lies beneath the clock which shows the time at half-past-four.

But when the clock device was first used on 7 January 1804 it did not include the scythe, and the clock showed the time as seven-and-a-half minutes past six, later changed to six minutes past six, which was then the average time for commencing publication. The device sometimes appeared with theatre bills and leaders on the back page, and sometimes at the bottom of a column with only the time of publication underneath. Before and after the use of the device, the actual time of publication was printed—the hour, presumably, being the time at which delivery of copies to the newsboys began.

As from 7 February 1911, the clock device headed the leader page, and on 1 January 1949 a new version of the device, designed by Reynolds Stone, appeared. This was discontinued from 3 May 1966 when news was printed on the front page for the first time.

Today's clock device loosely follows Reynolds Stone's design, but the time on the clock has been altered to 4.30 to indicate the earlier morning time of publication; 4.30am is the last possible time *The Times* can go to print to call itself a morning paper; any time later would make it an evening paper. Just another sign of 'the times'.

Tipp-Ex®

Though it has been said that diamonds are a girl's best friend, many typists will tell you that their best friend is Tipp-Ex, for since the introduction of this completely new way of effacing typing errors, millions of people no longer have to tolerate the use of crumb-producing rubbers; they now reach out instead for the strip of Tipp-Ex.

The product was invented in 1959 by Mr Wolfgang Dabisch, of Eltville/Rhein who also coined the name from *tippen*, a German word which means to touch something with the fingertips and which also has the meaning of 'to type', and the Latin *ex* meaning out.

Tipp-Ex was registered on 6 July, 1962, in Germany, and is now registered all over the world. Many other products have followed, such as Foto Copy Fluid, Super Plastic Film, Fingertip Moistener, correction pens, and so on, all under the brand Tipp-Ex produced by Tipp-Ex Vertrieb GmbH & Company, KG Frankfurt/Main.

So widely recognised has this product become that a letter was received at the Company's Frankfurt office with nothing but a strip of Tipp-Ex paper pasted on the envelope, showing the print on the back instead of an address. The letter had been sent from Algeria and, although in Arabic, it was recognised as praise indeed for Tipp-Ex. In many places overseas, on his visits, the Company's Managing Director is known as Mr Tipp-Ex!

Triumph International

Social conventions of the late nineteenth century deemed corsets a part of feminine elegance one did not talk about. So when 'Triumph' became a registered trademark in 1902, the name was apt; now the hushed-up garment could be called by name and an essential step towards the development of brand merchandise had been achieved.

The company was founded in 1886 by corsetry-maker Johann Gottfried Spiesshofer and merchant Michael Braun in a small workshop at Heubach/Wuerttemberg, Germany. It expanded rapidly, always adapting to the needs of current fashion.

In 1905 the tunic-dress created by a Paris fashion designer Monsieur P. Poiret, to be worn without corsets, led to the invention of the girdle. But not until after the First World War in 1922, when women's new spirit of life induced a further change in fashion and 'being free' necessitated doing away with any type of corset, was the first Triumph brassiere placed on the home market.

Over the years, Johann Spiesshofer's son Fritz and Michael Braun's two sons, Curt and Dr Herbert Braun, joined the management. By 1939, twenty plants apart from the factory in Heubach were producing bras, corselets and girdles. In 1953, now Europe's largest foundation maker, the company changed its name to Triumph International.

In 1964, Günther Spiesshofer, grandson of the founder, took charge of the company's overseas areas. What began as, and still is, a family partnership from Germany today runs production plants in four continents while its distribution system spans the globe. Indeed, Triumph International.

Velcro

This registered trademark comes from the words *velours* and *crochet* to indicate hooked velvet. It also seems to work as easily in English—velvet crochet. The idea of this touch-and-close fastener is really copied from nature—from the burdock burr, sometimes called sticky bobs by boys. Velcro was invented in Switzerland by a man named de Mestral.

It was from studying the way in which those annoying burdock burrs clung to his clothes (and his dog) after a hunting trip in the Swiss mountains, that the inventor of Velcro devised this versatile modern fastening. Touch the hook side of a piece of Velcro to the loop side, and they cling together like burrs. Among many thousands of applications, its use in hospitals, on medical dressings and on clothes for the elderly or disabled, as well as sportswear, is invaluable.

Virtual worldwide acceptance of the trademark, first registered in 1959, has been helped by the fact that Velcro is easy to say in most languages.

Vicks

The idea for this trademark came to Lunsford Richardson, founder of the Vick Chemical Company, in the 1890s when he saw a magazine advertisement for Vick's Seeds. Vick also happened to be his brother-in-law's name and this was just what he wanted, he decided—a short name, easy to remember.

Lunsford Richardson was born in 1854 near Selma, North Carolina. His widowed mother worked so hard to send him to Davidson College that Richardson pushed himself to compress four years of college into three. Although he was interested in chemistry, he majored in Latin; he also won the Greek medal, the debates medal and graduated with highest honours in 1875.

He was first a school teacher, and then a pharmacist. In 1890 he moved to Greensboro and bought the Porter & Tate Drugstore. Dr Porter's nephew, a clerk at the drugstore, was William Sidney Porter, who years later became the famous short story writer, O. Henry. Greensboro was a small market town where most customers were farmers who rarely consulted a doctor for simple ailments, but asked Richardson to prescribe medicines for their needs instead.

Over the years he developed a number of these home remedies which he sold under the name Vicks. One of these he developed especially for his son who was known as a 'croupy baby'. It was a vaporizing salve for colds, incorporating menthol, then a new and little-known drug from Japan. This salve, later named Vicks VaporRub, became the product on which the future Vick business was to be built.

In 1905, Richardson founded the Vick Family Remedies Company which handled nothing but his own twenty-one Vicks products, the predecessor of today's Richardson-Merrell Incorporated. By concentrating his efforts on those twenty-one products Richardson hoped eventually to realise his dream—to make the Vick registered trademark a household word in the United States and around the world.

Viyella

This fabric derived its name from Via Gellia, a leafy valley near Matlock Bath in Derbyshire where, around 1890,

William Hollins & Company bought a factory. The local inhabitants called the valley 'Vi Jella' and from this came the name of one of the most coveted cloths in the world.

Just over a hundred years before this, in 1784 when William Hollins founded the company, it produced yarn for the hosiery trade. But many years later two brothers, Robert and James Sisson, who had worked in the company's mill near Sherwood Forest since they were nine years old, were given a new task. It involved their trying to produce a yarn blend of two natural fibres—wool and cotton.

The brothers tried every method they knew to mix and prepare wool and cotton that could be woven into cloth, then they would rush the results off to their weavers in Scotland. One by one the experiments failed until news came that a Scottish company had found a way to weave the cloth. But only perfection would satisfy the brothers; they spent yet another painstaking year experimenting. By the end of 1893, more than 100 years after the company had been formed, it was clear they were to have a greater success than they had ever dared to hope for—an unshrinkable cloth which, because of its association with the valley Via Gellia, became known in over 60 countries as Viyella.

Johnnie Walker

This cheerful, Regency figure, complete with top hat, eyeglass and cane, stepping out with a purposeful stride, the trademark of the Scotch whisky firm, is from a sketch of the founder himself.

Its story began in 1820 when John Walker, a young Ayrshire man, bought a grocery, wine and spirit business in King Street, Kilmarnock, and expanded rapidly. His go-ahead son, Alexander, later reached overseas markets through the nineteenth-century Merchant Venturer system, whereby goods were entrusted to the captain of a ship who would sell them on commission at the best price he could get. In 1888 Alexander's son, Alexander, joined the company, and later received a knighthood. It was Sir Alexander Walker who, in 1908, with new sales ideas, decided to incorporate a portrait of his grandfather into the advertising scheme. He commissioned Tom Browne, a celebrated commercial artist, to depict the founder of the firm as he might have appeared in 1820. Sir Alexander's colleague, Lord Stevenson, scribbled alongside the finished sketch the catch-phrase that was to become famous: 'Johnnie Walker born 1820—still going strong'. This company has claimed use of the words 'Johnnie Walker' since 1880 and the use of the striding figure device since 1910.

This original sketch was miraculously rescued unharmed from Walker's premises which were bombed during the Second World War and it remains a prized possession of the company today.

The Wellcome Foundation

The unicorn, as a symbol of healing, was first registered in 1908 by Burroughs Wellcome & Company. The unicorn itself never existed but dust ground from its supposed horn was part of the equipment of the European pharmacist until the eighteenth-century. The long horns that were exhibited under this guise were really the tusks of the narwhal. The horn itself was believed to break into a sweat when placed near food containing poison, and this way of testing food continued in the royal household of France until 1789. A potion made from the dust was prescribed to cure poisons, fevers, bites of scorpions and mad dogs, falling sickness, worms, fluxes, loss of memory and the plague. Water in which a unicorn horn had rested was drunk as a medicine.

The design for the unicorn trademark was actually determined by Henry Wellcome and only after much correspondence. Again and again he criticised and compared the sketches drawn by different artists. He insisted the design should portray delicacy and refinement, grace with virility and verve, and the possibility of fleetness and an expression of alertness—characteristics of the unicorn. The drawing by a Mr Scrobie of the College of Heralds was eventually accepted, with slight reservations. Today, the unicorn symbol (slightly modified in 1969) in conjunction with the word 'Wellcome' is recognised throughout the world.

'Tabloid' was another trademark thought up by Henry Wellcome and registered in 1884, from the words 'tablet' and 'alkaloid'. In 1903, Wellcome went to court to defend Tabloid as a Burroughs Wellcome trademark and finally won the case. Tabloid is one of the most distinguished of all registered trademarks and is one of the very few proprietary names to go into the *Oxford Dictionary*. Despite the derivation of Tabloid, the name could be used as a trademark for any of the Wellcome Foundation's products, not just medicines. It was even used for compressed tea tablets which were taken on expeditions. Some of the Tabloid tea was discovered in perfect condition approximately 50 years after it had been stored at Dawson City during the Klondike gold rush!

White Horse Whisky

Sir Peter Jeffrey Mackie Bt (1855-1924) was the last descendant of the Mackies, an old Stirlingshire family who had owned property in Edinburgh since 1650. Near the family home was one of the most famous of ancient inns—The White Horse Cellar in Canongate.

It was this historic family connection that inspired Peter Mackie to choose the same name for his whisky when he succeeded his uncle in 1890. History shows that officers of Bonnie Prince Charlie's army relaxed off duty at The White Horse Inn during the rebellion of 1745.

Peter built up the business into one of the great whisky firms of the world, and officially registered the name White Horse Cellar Scotch Whisky in 1891. Some people may wonder why underneath the famous White Horse symbol on the label is stated 'Estab 1742'. This is because, although the Mackie family were established as merchants and property owners as far back as 1651, according to the historian Ross Wilson 'To some extent the business can be dated back to 1742 when it was "founded" in a sense. It was then owned by a man of the name of Johnson, and consisted of ten small and separate bothies at Lagavulin on the Island of Islay—smuggling bothies, of course—where "moonlight" was made. All these were subsequently absorbed into the one establishment.'

The small label on the back of every bottle of White Horse shows the original White Horse Cellar in the Canongate of Edinburgh with a four-in-hand stage coach leaving for London.

In Edinburgh today, if one walks down the Royal Mile from the Castle to Holyroodhouse, the beautifully preserved White Horse Close can be seen. A plaque at the entrance says it was named after the white palfrey which bore Mary Queen of Scots up and down that same Royal Mile, and at the back of the Close can be seen the building which was the inn which gave its name to the whisky.

Woolmark

Because wool was being threatened by a manmade competitor, rayon, wool-growers in 1937 launched the International Wool Secretariat. But at that time, wool had no international trademark and when the time came, designing a trademark had its problems. The mark had to be patented in 90 countries, and legal searches showed that many symbols suggested as the new sign for wool could not be protected.

So, bearing in mind the registration complications, and that confusion with any existing symbol must be avoided, the International Wool Secretariat held an international competition to find a suitable design. The winning designer was Francisco Saroglio, art director of a Milan advertising agency. His Woolmark emblem was chosen from 86 submissions by an international jury. Though not strictly representational, the design resembles the soft drape of wool; it is simple enough to reduce to a very small size without distortion, it cannot be mistaken for any existing registered trademarks and it has no unexpected significance—religious, political, or sexual—anywhere in the world.

The Woolmark quality symbol was introduced in 1964. Today, about 350 million Woolmark labels are used every year by more than 14,000 licensees in 51 countries. And over 400 million people can, as they buy their clothes, knitwear, hand-knitting yarns, upholstery, carpets, and much more besides, recognise the quality symbol for pure new wool—the Woolmark.

Acknowledgements

The author would like to offer her sincere thanks to all who have supplied information for this book, to legal, patent and trademark departments, librarians and numerous public relations consultants. The assistance of the following owners of various trademarks, names and symbols, have been of special value:

Aquascutum Ltd, London
Barclays Bank, Lombard Street, London
Bass Ltd, London
BAT (UK & Export) Woking, Surrey
Beaverbrook Newspapers Ltd, London
Birds Eye Foods Ltd, Walton-on-Thames, Surrey
Bostik Ltd, Leicester
Bovril Bureau, London
Bryant & May Ltd, London
Edward R. Buck & Sons, Stockport, Cheshire
James Burrough Ltd, London
Carreras Rothmans Ltd, 64 Pall Mall, London
Cologne Perfumery Ltd, Basingstoke, Hampshire
CPC (UK) & (Europe), Brussels, Belgium
Cussons, London
Cuxson, Gerrard & Co Ltd, Warley, West Midlands
W. David & Sons, Whetstone, London
John Dickinson Stationery, Hemel Hempstead, Herts
The Drambuie Liqueur Co Ltd, Edinburgh
EMI Records Ltd, Hayes, Middlesex
Esso Petroleum Co Ltd, London
General Foods Ltd, Banbury, Oxon
Glaxo Holdings, Clarges Street, London
Arthur Guinness Son & Co, 10 Albemarle Street, London
Harris Tweed Association Ltd, Inverness
H. J. Heinz & Co, Hayes, Middlesex
Hiram Walker (International) SA, Montreaux, Switzerland
Hoover Ltd, Greenford, Middlesex
ICI, Wexham Road, Slough
International Wool Secretariat, 99 Carlton Gardens, London
Jaguar-Rover-Triumph Ltd, Coventry
Kiwi Products (UK) Ltd, Yateley, Surrey
Kosset Carpets, Halifax, West Yorkshire
LEGO (UK) Ltd, Wrexham, Clwyd
Lloyds Bank Ltd, Lombard Street, London

Marks & Spencer Ltd, Baker Street, London
Marmite Ltd, Burton-on-Trent, Staffordshire
Mettoy Playcraft Ltd, Northampton
Michelin Tyre Co Ltd, London
Midland Bank Ltd, 41 Silver Street Head, Sheffield
National Benzole Co Ltd, 195 Knightsbridge, London
Nestlé & Co, Croydon, Surrey
Nicholas Laboratories Ltd, 225 Bath Road, Slough
The Observer, London
R. Paterson & Sons Ltd, Glasgow
Penguin Books Ltd, Kings Road, London
Pepsico, Feltham, Middlesex
Pifco Ltd, Failsworth, Manchester
J. R. Phillips, Avonmouth, Bristol
John Player & Sons, Nottingham
Quaker Oats Ltd, Southall, Middlesex
Rentokil Ltd, East Grinstead, West Sussex
Richardson-Merrell Ltd, Slough, Berks
James Robertson & Sons, Droylsden, Manchester
Rolls-Royce Ltd, Derby
St Ives Ltd, Trowbridge, Wilts
Selectus Ltd, Stoke-on-Trent
Shell International Petroleum Co Ltd, London
Spar (UK) Ltd, Harrow, Middlesex
Texaco Ltd, 1 Knightsbridge Green, London
Thermos Ltd, Brentwood, Essex
The Times Newspapers Ltd, (Archivist J. G. Phillips),
    London
Tipp-Ex Vertrieb GmbH & Co, KG Frankfurt/Main, West
    Germany
Triumph International Ltd, Swindon, Wilts
Umbro International (Footwear) Ltd, Stockport, Cheshire
United Rum Merchants Ltd, 97 Tooley Street, London
John Walker & Sons Ltd, St James Street, London
Wander Ltd, King's Langley, Hertfordshire
The Wellcome Foundation Ltd, Euston Road, London
White Horse Distillers Ltd, Borron Street, Glasgow
The Wiggins Teape Group Ltd, Basingstoke, Hampshire
William Hollins & Co Ltd, Somercotes, Derby
Wolverine World Wide Inc, Rockford, Michigan, USA